W9-APM-752

DISASTER ZONE
EARTHQUAKES

by Cari Meister

Ideas for Parents and Teachers

Pogo Books let children practice reading informational text while introducing them to nonfiction features such as headings, labels, sidebars, maps, and diagrams, as well as a table of contents, glossary, and index.

Carefully leveled text with a strong photo match offers early fluent readers the support they need to succeed.

Before Reading

- "Walk" through the book and point out the various nonfiction features. Ask the student what purpose each feature serves.
- Look at the glossary together. Read and discuss the words.

Read the Book

- Have the child read the book independently.
- Invite him or her to list questions that arise from reading.

After Reading

- Discuss the child's questions. Talk about how he or she might find answers to those questions.
- Prompt the child to think more. Ask: Have you ever been in an earthquake? How would you describe the experience?

Pogo Books are published by Jump!
5357 Penn Avenue South
Minneapolis, MN 55419
www.jumplibrary.com

Library of Congress Cataloging-in-Publication Data

Meister, Cari, author.
 Earthquakes / by Cari Meister.
    pages cm. – (Disaster zone)
 Summary: "Carefully leveled text and engaging full-color photos introduce early fluent readers to the science behind earthquakes, including where and why earthquakes happen and how to stay safe when the ground starts to shake. Includes activity, glossary, and index."–Provided by publisher.
 Audience: Ages 7-10.
 Includes index.
 ISBN 978-1-62031-220-9 (hardcover: alk. paper) –
 ISBN 978-1-62031-265-0 (paperback) –
 ISBN 978-1-62496-307-0 (ebook)
 1. Earthquakes–Juvenile literature.
 2. Plate tectonics–Juvenile literature. I. Title.
 QE534.3.M45 2016
 551.22–dc23

                                        2014042539

Series Editor: Jenny Fretland VanVoorst
Series Designer: Anna Peterson
Photo Researcher: Anna Peterson

Photo Credits: Alamy, 10-11; Corbis, 4, 23; Getty, 6-7, 16-17, 20-21; National Geographic, 14-15; NigelSpiers/Shutterstock.com, 13; Prometheus72/Shutterstock.com, 1, 12; Shutterstock, 3, 8-9, 18, 19; Thinkstock, cover, 5.

Printed in the United States of America at Corporate Graphics in North Mankato, Minnesota.

TABLE OF CONTENTS

CHAPTER 1

IT'S AN EARTHQUAKE!

Imagine you are on vacation in San Francisco. You are at a restaurant having lunch.

All of a sudden, the ground starts to shake. Dishes fall to the floor. Wow! What is going on?

It's an earthquake!

Luckily, it's a small one. After a few **tremors**, things go back to normal.

So what just happened?

Earthquakes are sudden shifts of the earth's surface. The earth's surface is called the **crust**. It is made up of large pieces of earth called **plates**. The plates float on a sea of liquid rock.

WHERE ARE THEY?

There are seven major plates. The area around the Pacific Plate has the most earthquakes.

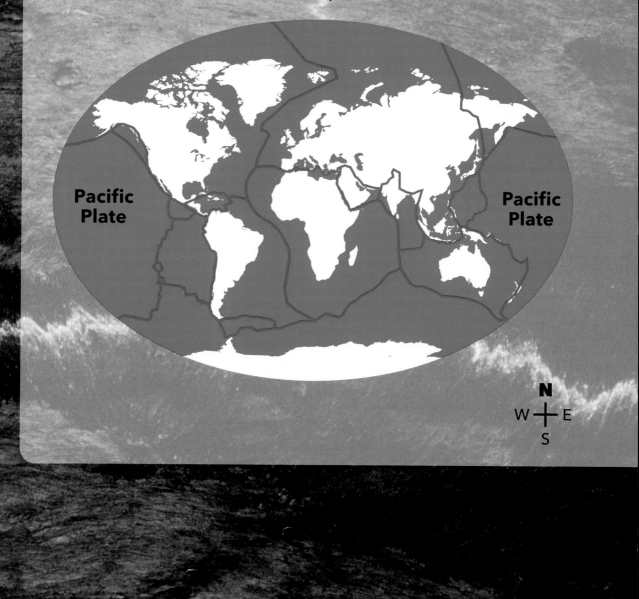

Pacific Plate

Pacific Plate

N
W — E
S

Imagine a bowl of milk covered in corn flakes. Move the bowl a little. What happens to the flakes? They bump against one another. Plates bump against each other in much the same way.

These bumps cause the crust to crack. The cracking sends out energy that we feel as an earthquake.

DID YOU KNOW?

Sometimes a quake cracks the crust under the ocean. This can create a giant wave called a **tsunami**.

Earthquakes often happen near **fault lines**. These are places where there are breaks in the crust.

WHERE DO THEY HAPPEN?

Almost 90 percent of quakes happen in a region called the **Ring of Fire**. It is an area where many plates meet.

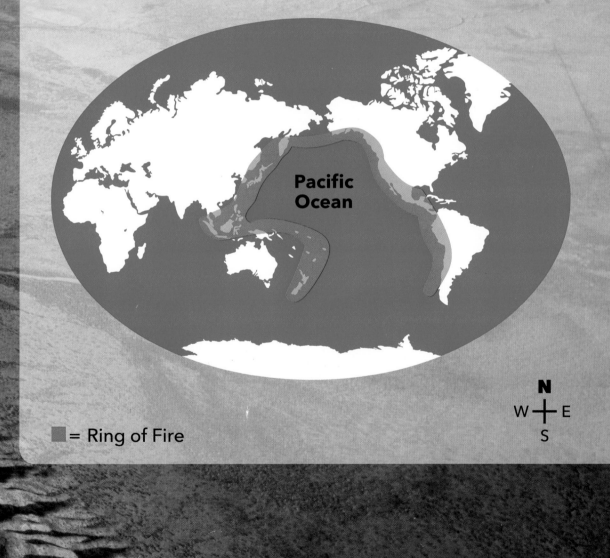

Pacific Ocean

■ = Ring of Fire

N
W ┼ E
S

CHAPTER 2

DEADLY EARTHQUAKES

There are more than 500,000 earthquakes per year. Most are so small you cannot feel them. But sometimes they are deadly.

During bad ones, buildings, bridges, and roads collapse. Gas lines break. Fires start. People die.

The deadliest quake happened in 1556 in China. It killed about 830,000 people.

In 2010, an earthquake in Haiti killed more than 200,000 people.

To compare earthquakes, scientists use two scales.

The **Richter scale** measures the size and strength of a quake. This is its **magnitude**.

The **Mercalli scale** measures the **intensity** of a quake. This is the amount of damage it causes.

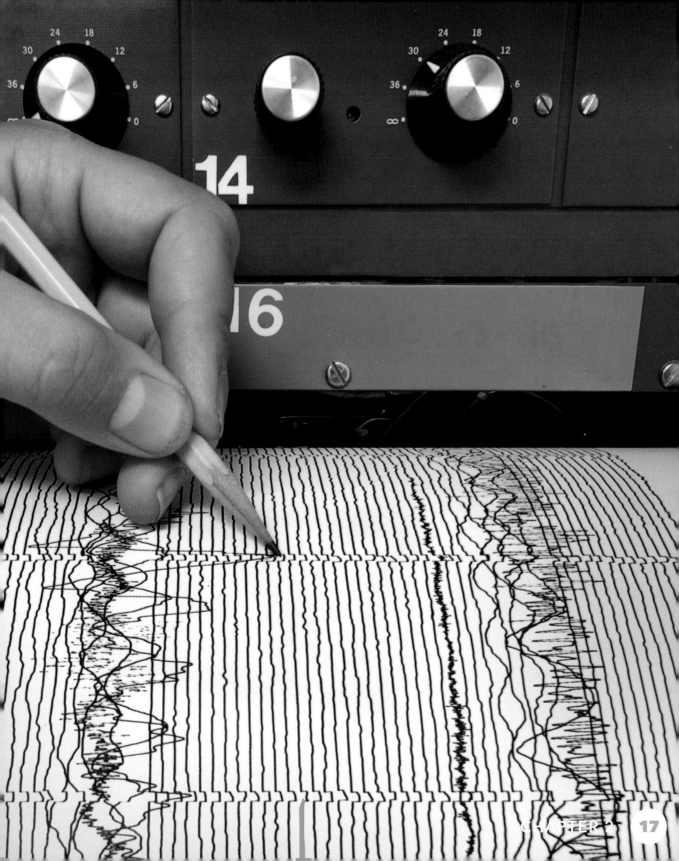

CHAPTER 3

STAYING SAFE

Today many buildings are built to be "earthquake safe." They can move and sway during a quake. Being able to bend makes them less likely to break.

Taiwan's Taipei 101 skyscraper was built to survive an earthquake. In 2002, a huge quake rocked the island. The tower stood tall!

Taipei 101

How can you stay safe in an earthquake? If you are at school, you may be asked to go under your desk. If you are outside, move away from anything that can fall on you.

Disasters can happen anytime. But be prepared, and you can stay safe in an earthquake.

DID YOU KNOW?

An emergency kit is helpful in any disaster. It should include:

- Water
- Canned or dried food (and a can opener)
- First aid kit
- Cell phone and charger
- Radio
- Blankets

ACTIVITIES & TOOLS

CRACK THE CRUST

What You Need:
- A thin wood stick

❶ Hold the stick horizontally with your hands on each end.

❷ Bend down on both ends until the stick breaks in the middle.

The wood stick is like the earth's crust. When the stick breaks, it releases the stress you have put on it, similar to the way moving plates put pressure on the earth's crust, causing it to crack.

CORN FLAKE PLATES

What You Need:
- A bowl, corn flakes, milk

❶ Put milk and corn flakes in a bowl.

❷ Gently jostle the bowl.

The corn flakes are like the earth's plates. When you move the bowl, the corn flakes rub up and bump into each other, just like the earth's plates do.

GLOSSARY

crust: The outer layer of the earth.

fault lines: Crack in the earth's crust.

intensity: How much damage an earthquake causes.

magnitude: How powerful an earthquake is.

Mercalli scale: The scale that assesses the intensity of an earthquake.

plates: Large pieces of crust that float on a sea of liquid rock.

Richter scale: The scale that assesses the magnitude of an earthquake.

Ring of Fire: The region bordering the Pacific Ocean where there are a lot of volcanoes and earthquakes.

tremors: The shaking movements on the ground caused by an earthquake.

tsunami: A giant wave caused by underwater movement of Earth's crust.

INDEX

TO LEARN MORE

Learning more is as easy as 1, 2, 3.

1) Go to www.factsurfer.com

2) Enter "earthquakes" into the search box.

3) Click the "Surf" to see a list of websites.

With factsurfer, finding more information is just a click away.